BONITA'S KITCHEN

A Little Taste of Home

Library and Archives Canada Cataloguing in Publication

Title: Bonita's kitchen : a little taste of home / Bonita Hussey.
Names: Hussey, Bonita - author.
Description: Includes index.
Identifiers: Canadiana 20200321560 | ISBN 9781989417218 (softcover)
Subjects: LCSH: Baking. | LCGFT: Cookbooks.
Classification: LCC TX763 .H88 2020 | DDC 641.81/5—dc23

Design and layout: Todd Manning
Front and back cover photos: Raymond Hussey
Editor: Stephanie Porter
Copy editor: Iona Bulgin

Printed in Canada

We acknowledge the financial support of the Government of Newfoundland and Labrador through the Department of Tourism, Culture and Recreation.

Newfoundland Labrador

Funded by the Government of Canada   Financé par le gouvernement du Canada   Canada

BONITA'S KITCHEN

A Little Taste of Home

Bonita Hussey

BOULDER
BOOKS

Dedicated to Raymond Hussey, my husband, partner, cameraman, producer, and friend. Raymond has spent endless hours helping with Bonita's Kitchen, putting his hobbies on the back shelf.

TABLE OF CONTENTS

vii   Introduction

ix   Conversion Tables, Definitions, and Notes on Ingredients

YEAST BREADS

2   White Bread

3   Whole Wheat Bread

4   Cinnamon Raisin Bread

6   Gluten-Free Bread

7   Hamburger Buns

8   Molasses and Raisin Bread

11   Multigrain Bread

12   Oatmeal Honey Bread

14   Pizza Dough

15   Pumpernickel Bread

17   Salmon Bread Roll

18   Toutons

20   Gluten-Free Toutons

SWEET DOUGH

22   Christmas Fruit Bread

24   Cinnamon Blueberry Sticky Rolls

26   Hot Cross Buns

QUICK BREADS, SCONES, AND MUFFINS

30   Banana Almond Spice Bread

33   Blueberry Scones with Lemon Glaze

34   Date Nut Loaf

36   Hard Bread (Hard Tack)

37   Gluten-Free Hard Bread

38   Molasses Buns

39   Partridgeberry Muffins

40   Pumpkin Carrot Walnut Muffins with Cream Cheese Frosting

43   Soda Bread

COOKIES AND SQUARES

46 Apple Squares with Toffee Sauce
49 Sweet Apple Wedges
50 Apricot Squares
52 Gingerbread House *or* Cookies
54 Lemon Crumbles
55 Oatmeal Raisin Cookies

CAKES

58 Carrot Cake with Cream Cheese Icing
59 Dark Rum Fruit Cake
61 Double Chocolate Cake
62 Pound Cake with Coconut Butter Icing
64 Tomato Soup Cake with Buttercream Icing
67 Upside-Down Rhubarb Cake

PIES AND PASTRIES

70 Coconut Cream Pie
72 Key Lime Pie
74 Lemon Meringue Pie
76 Maple Butter Tarts
78 Pumpkin Spice Cream Cheese Pie

OTHER DESSERTS

82 Apple Flips
84 Baked Partridgeberry Pudding
85 Blueberry Bread Pudding with Caramel Sauce
86 Blueberry Cobbler
87 Blueberry Shortcake
88 Easter Pudding with White Cream Sauce
90 Lemon Pudding
92 Meringue Bowls with Rhubarb-Berry Filling
94 Peach Cobbler

INTRODUCTION

Welcome to Bonita's Kitchen!

I'm excited to share my love of baking with you. The recipes that I have selected for this collection are some of my all-time favourite baking recipes—and they are all so easy to make.

When I was 18 years old, I worked in a small bakery in my community of Upper Island Cove, Newfoundland and Labrador, making breads, buns, cakes, cookies, and pies. During that time, I worked beside my sister-in-law Viola, who taught me so much. In that bakery began my lifelong hobby and passion for baking. Over the years I've tried my hand at dozens, maybe hundreds, of different desserts and loved every one of them.

But more than any other kitchen creation, I love to make bread—any type of bread—because I find it so relaxing. I also love to teach, and share.

My recipes are designed to be accessible and straightforward. The ingredients list is simple; you will have most of these ingredients in your cupboard already. The method is step-by-step and clearly explained to guide you through a successful bake. Most of the bread recipes follow a similar method to make it easier for you.

This book is designed to help the new baker get started. It also has lots of treats and tips for more experienced bakers.

So please, sit back, make yourself a cup of tea, and enjoy.

1 cup = 250 ml
3/4 cup = 190 ml
2/3 cup = 170 ml
½ cup = 125 ml
⅓ cup = 85 ml
¼ cup = 65 ml

1 tbsp = 15 ml
1 tsp = 5 ml
½ tsp = 2.5 ml
¼ tsp = 1.25 ml

425°F = 220°C
400°F = 200°C
375°F = 190°C
350°F = 180°C
325°F = 165°C
300°F = 150°C
275°F = 140°C
250°F = 120°C
225°F = 110°C
220°F = 105°C
200°F = 95°C
175°F = 80°C

11 in = 28 cm
10 in = 25.5 cm
9 in = 23 cm
8 in = 20.5 cm
2 in = 5 cm
1 in = 2.5 cm

CONVERSION TABLES

The recipes in this book give measurements in cups, tablespoons, teaspoons, ounces, and inches. Temperatures are given in Fahrenheit, still the most popular scale for most North American cooks. Those who prefer to work in millilitres, centimetres, or Celsius may refer to the conversion tables at left for assistance.

A FEW HELPFUL DEFINITIONS

CUBE: to cut uniform ½-inch squares.

DICE: to cut into uniform pieces, usually ⅛ to ¼ inch.

FOLD: to combine a light mixture, such as beaten egg whites, with a heavy mixture, such as cake batter, without the loss of air. Heavy ingredients are folded directly into the centre of the light ingredients with a spatula and pulled toward the edge of the bowl or with your hand.

KNEADING: to push down into dough and fold inward by hand, releasing air, activating gluten, and eventually pulling the dough into a ball.

NOTES ON INGREDIENTS

Sugar: unless stated otherwise, sugar is white granulated.
Evaporated milk: can be standard or 2%; you may substitute any fresh milk or milk alternative (soy, almond, oatmeal, etc.), though this may slightly affect the flavour.
Milk: usually I use whole milk; you may substitute any fresh milk or milk alternative. Again, this may slightly affect the flavour.
Butter: unless otherwise noted, use salted butter; you may substitute margarine. (If using unsalted butter, add ½ to 1 teaspoon salt to the recipe.)
Juice: orange, lime, and lemon juice is always better freshly squeezed; substitute with bottled juice as required.
Oatmeal: use quick or rolled oats; large-flake oats should be chopped or ground in a food processor unless you prefer the chunkier texture. Do not use steel-cut oats unless indicated.
Cream cheese: use full-fat or light.
Sour cream: use full-fat or light.

Whole Wheat Bread

YEAST BREADS

WHITE BREAD

Makes 3 loaves

8½ cups all-purpose white flour

2 tbsp white sugar

½ to 1 tsp sea salt

2 tbsp traditional or fast-rising yeast

3 cups warm water

2 tbsp melted butter

BONITA'S TIPS
Add more water or flour as required to bring the dough together as you mix it before the first rise.

Have all ingredients measured and ready to use before you start.

Do not deflate the dough on its last rising; you need the air to stay in the dough when shaping it into balls.

In a large bowl, combine 8 cups of the flour, 1 tablespoon of the sugar, and sea salt.

In another bowl, combine the yeast with the warm water and 1 tablespoon of the sugar. Set aside to rise for 5 minutes.

Using a wooden spoon, make a hole in the flour mixture and pour in the yeast mixture. Add the melted butter. Mix all ingredients with a wooden spoon or a stand mixer until thick. Gradually add up to ½ cup flour as required to bring the dough together.

Knead using a stand mixer's dough hook attachment or by hand until the dough is smooth, elastic, and no longer sticky. You should hear the dough cracking as you fold it. Work the dough into a ball.

Sprinkle additional flour over the dough. Cover with parchment paper and a tea towel. Let the dough rise in a warm place for about 30 minutes. Knead it down for 2 or 3 minutes. Let it rise another 30 minutes but **do not deflate**.

Preheat oven to 350°F.

Cut the dough into 9 pieces and form each piece into a ball. Grease the bread pans with butter or oil. Place 3 balls in each pan. The dough can also be shaped into individual rolls. Cover and let rise 30 minutes in a warm place.

Bake 30 to 35 minutes or until golden brown. Remove from the pans and let cool on a cooling rack. Glaze bread with butter and cover with the tea towel to cool.

WHOLE WHEAT BREAD

Makes 3 loaves

7½ cups whole wheat flour

1 tsp sea salt

3 cups warm water

⅓ cup honey or 2 tbsp white sugar

1 tbsp fast-rising or traditional yeast

2 tbsp melted butter or oil

In a large bowl, combine 7 cups of the flour and sea salt.

In a small bowl, combine the warm water, yeast, and honey or sugar. Set aside to rise for 5 minutes.

Add the yeast mixture to the flour and combine, using a wooden spoon or a stand mixer. Add the melted butter and continue to mix.

Mix in the remaining ½ cup flour as needed until the dough starts to pull away from the sides of the bowl. Knead 10 minutes; form the dough into a ball.

Cover with parchment paper and a tea towel and let rise in a warm place for 30 minutes.

Uncover the dough and knead for a few minutes. Cover again and let rise another 20 to 30 minutes.

Do not deflate the dough. Grease 3 bread pans with butter or oil. Rub a little butter on your hands and shape the dough into 3 balls or one long piece per pan; place in the pans.

Cover with parchment paper and a tea towel and let rise another 20 to 30 minutes, until the dough is just over the top of the pans. Do not over-rise.

Preheat oven to 350°F. Bake 30 to 35 minutes. Remove the bread from the pans and place on a cooling rack.

BONITA'S TIPS
Freeze the loaves you will not use immediately after they have been cooled completely.

Brush melted butter over the top of the warm bread, cover with parchment paper and a tea towel, and let cool to room temperature before bagging. This prevents moisture build-up in the bag before freezing or storing.

CINNAMON RAISIN BREAD

Makes 3 loaves

1 recipe white bread
(page 2)

1 cup brown sugar

½ cup or more raisins

¼ cup cinnamon

¼ cup melted butter

Follow the method for white bread (page 2) to the first rise.

In a small bowl, mix the brown sugar, raisins, and cinnamon. Set aside.

After the dough finishes its first rise, turn it out onto a floured cutting board and cut into 3 pieces. Use your fingers or a rolling pin to flatten each piece, spreading the dough as far as it will go.

Sprinkle ⅓ of the cinnamon-raisin mixture over each piece of dough and drizzle the melted butter evenly over the top. Roll the dough away from you and place one dough roll in each of 3 bread pans.

Cover loaves with parchment paper and a large tea towel. Place in a warm spot in the kitchen until the dough rises by half the size you started with, about 30 minutes.

Preheat oven to 350°F.

Bake 30 minutes or until golden brown. Remove from the pans and place on a cooling rack.

Glaze loaves with butter while hot, then cover with parchment paper and a tea towel to soften the crust.

BONITA'S TIPS
Letting bread cool on a cooling rack prevents it from getting moist on the bottom.

Let bread cool totally before bagging; freeze to keep bread fresh longer.

GLUTEN-FREE BREAD

Makes 1 loaf

3 cups gluten-free white flour

3 tbsp white sugar

1¼ tsp sea salt

2 tsp xanthan gum

½ cup warm water

2 tsp fast-rising or traditional yeast

½ cup warm milk

4 tbsp melted butter

3 large eggs

In a large bowl, combine the flour, 2 tablespoons of the sugar, sea salt, and xanthan gum.

In a small bowl, combine the warm water, yeast, and 1 tablespoon sugar. Set aside to rise for 5 minutes, then add to the flour mixture and stir.

Gradually add the warm milk while beating using a wooden spoon or a hand or stand mixer. The mixture will be crumbly at first, but will come together as all the milk is added. While continuing to beat, add the butter, then the eggs, one at a time. Scrape the sides and bottom of the bowl, then beat at high speed for an additional 3 minutes to make a smooth, thick batter.

Cover the bowl and let rise for 45 minutes to 1 hour in a warm area in your kitchen.

Scrape down the sides and bottom of the bowl, gently deflating the batter to remove the air. Grease a 9 x 5-inch loaf pan. Scoop the dough carefully into the pan, using a spatula or your oiled fingers to smooth the top of the batter.

Cover with greased parchment paper and let rise for about 45 to 60 minutes, until the loaf surface is barely above the rim of the pan.

Preheat oven to 350°F. Bake 35 to 40 minutes or until golden brown.

Remove from the pan and place on a cooling rack. Add a little butter to the top, cover for a few minutes with parchment paper and a tea towel before slicing.

Fried toutons: Take a small amount of the risen dough and shape it into a palm-sized cake, flattened to about 1 inch thick. Heat the frying pan on medium heat and melt 1 tablespoon butter. Fry the dough about 4 minutes on each side or until golden brown. Serve with jam or molasses and a cup of tea.

HAMBURGER BUNS

Makes 4 to 6 buns

2 tsp fast-rising or traditional yeast

1 cup warm water

1 tsp white sugar

2 cups all-purpose white flour

½ tsp sea salt

1 large egg

1 tbsp melted butter

Olive oil

Sesame seeds (optional)

BONITA'S TIPS
This recipe can be doubled but **do not increase the amount of yeast**.

After buns have cooled, store in a freezer bag in the freezer to preserve freshness.

Instead of sesame seeds, try topping buns with cheese or poppy seeds.

Cutting a cross into the top of the bread dough is optional; this is a Newfoundland tradition.

Preheat oven to 350°F.

In a small bowl, combine the warm water, yeast, and sugar. Set aside to rise for 5 minutes.

Combine the flour and sea salt in a large bowl. Add the lightly beaten egg and melted butter and stir to combine. Add the yeast mixture and use a wooden spoon or a stand mixer (with dough hook) to combine.

When the dough becomes difficult to mix, use your hand to knead, pulling the dough toward you and pushing downward. Use more warm water or flour as required to bring the dough together.

Cut the dough into 4 or 6 pieces and roll each into a ball. Place the balls on a pan lined with parchment paper. Cut a cross in the top of each bun, drizzle with olive oil, and top with optional sesame seeds. Cover with a tea towel and let rise for 10 minutes in a warm place.

Bake 25 to 30 minutes or until golden brown on top. Remove from the oven and move the buns to a cooling rack.

MOLASSES AND RAISIN BREAD

Makes 3 loaves

8½ cups all-purpose white flour

½ cup brown sugar

½ tsp sea salt

2½ cups raisins

2 tbsp cinnamon

½ tsp ground cloves

2 tbsp fast-rising or traditional yeast

¼ cup melted butter

2 cups warm water

¾ cup molasses

1 tsp vanilla

½ tbsp white sugar

BONITA'S TIPS
Sweet bread is a little heavier than white bread, so it will not rise quite the same.

Grease the tops of the bread with butter while hot, then cover with parchment paper and a tea towel to soften the tops. Allow to cool to room temperature.

In a large bowl, combine 8 cups of the flour, brown sugar, sea salt, raisins, cinnamon, and ground cloves.

In a small bowl, add the yeast to 1 cup warm water and the white sugar. Set aside to rise for 5 minutes.

In another small bowl, combine 1 cup warm water and the molasses.

Pour the yeast mixture over the dry ingredients. Add the warm water and molasses, melted butter, and vanilla. Mix using a wooden spoon or a stand mixer until the dough thickens. Add the remaining flour as required to bring the dough together. Knead the dough, adding more flour if necessary, until the dough is smooth, elastic, and no longer sticky. You should hear cracking sounds while folding the dough inward. Work the dough into a ball.

Sprinkle flour over the dough. Cut a ½-inch-deep cross into the top of the dough. Cover with parchment paper and a tea towel to keep the dough warm.

Let rise in a warm place for 30 minutes. Knead down for 2 minutes. Let rise another 30 minutes. This time **do not deflate the dough**. Cut into 9 pieces and roll each inward into a ball. Grease 3 loaf pans and place 3 balls in each pan.

Cover the loaves and let them rise for about 30 minutes, until the dough is half the size again.

Preheat oven to 350°F.

Bake for 30 to 40 minutes or until golden brown. Remove from the pans and cool on a cooling rack.

MULTIGRAIN BREAD

Makes 3 loaves

3 cups warm water

7½ cups multigrain flour

1 tbsp fast-rising or traditional yeast

⅓ cup honey or 2 tbsp sugar

¼ cup melted butter or oil + extra tbsp for hand, pans, and bread tops

1 tsp 12-grain cereal mixture (optional)

1 tsp sesame seeds

1 tsp flax seeds

1 tsp pumpkin or sunflower seeds

1 to 1½ tsp sea salt

BONITA'S TIPS

Cool bread completely before bagging to avoid moisture buildup.

Feel free to substitute whole wheat flour for half the multigrain flour.

In a small bowl, combine the yeast, warm water, and honey or sugar. Set aside to rise for 5 minutes.

In a large bowl, combine 7 cups of the flour, ½ teaspoon sesame seeds, ½ teaspoon flax seeds, ½ teaspoon pumpkin or sunflower seeds, and sea salt. Mix using a wooden spoon or a stand mixer. Add the butter and yeast, stirring continuously. Add more warm water if needed.

Continue mixing or kneading until the dough forms a ball and all the flour has been incorporated, about 10 minutes. Add up to ½ cup flour if required to bring the dough into a ball.

Cut a cross into the top of the dough ball. Cover with a lid (or parchment paper and a tea towel). Let rise in a warm place in the kitchen for 20 to 30 minutes.

Knead the dough. Cut another cross into the top of the dough, cover, and let rise another 20 to 30 minutes. After this second rise, **do not deflate the dough**. Cut into 3 pieces.

Using a little butter or oil on your hands, shape each piece of dough into 3 small balls (for one loaf) or a loaf. Oil 3 loaf pans and add the dough to each one. Brush the top with butter and sprinkle extra seeds on top. Cover the pans with parchment paper and place in a warm place to rise until double, about 20 to 30 minutes.

Preheat oven to 350°F. When the loaves have risen, bake for 30 to 35 minutes.

Remove the loaves from the oven and place on cooling racks. Brush a little melted butter on the loaves and cover for 5 minutes to soften. Allow to cool completely before bagging.

OATMEAL HONEY BREAD

Makes 2 loaves

2 cups all-purpose white flour

2 cups whole wheat flour

1 cup oatmeal

1 tsp sea salt

2 tsp fast-rising or traditional yeast

1 cup warm water

¼ cup honey or 2 tbsp sugar

2 tbsp melted butter

½ cup warmed milk

1 tbsp corn syrup

Combine 1½ cups of the flour, all of the whole wheat flour, oatmeal, and sea salt in a large bowl.

In a small bowl, combine the yeast with the warm water and honey. Set aside to rise for 5 minutes.

Make a hole in the flour mixture and pour in the yeast, melted butter, warm milk, and corn syrup. Mix all ingredients with a wooden spoon or a stand mixer until thick. Add the remaining ½ cup flour and continue to work the dough together. If required, add a little warm water.

Knead the dough, adding more flour, if necessary, until it is smooth, elastic, and no longer sticky. You should hear the dough cracking when folding it. Keep working the dough into a ball.

Dust the dough with flour, cut a cross in the top, and cover with parchment paper and a tea towel. Let rise in a warm place for 30 minutes, then knead it down. Let the dough rise for another 30 minutes. **Do not deflate**.

Grease 2 loaf pans. Cut the dough in half, and cut each half into 3 equal pieces. Form each piece into a ball. Place 3 balls in each pan. If you prefer, simply fold each half of the dough inward into a loaf shape and place in the pans.

Cover and set in a warm place to rise for about 30 minutes, until the dough rises by half.

Preheat oven to 350°F.

Bake for 30 to 35 minutes. Remove the loaves from the oven and place on cooling racks. Brush a little melted butter on each loaf and cover for 5 minutes to soften.

PIZZA DOUGH

For 1 pizza

½ cup warm water

1 tsp fast-rising or traditional yeast

½ tsp white sugar

1¼ cups all-purpose white flour

½ tsp sea salt

½ tsp onion powder

½ tsp garlic powder

½ tsp Italian seasoning

1 tsp olive oil

BONITA'S TIPS

If you like thin-crust pizza, use half the dough; freeze the other half in a freezer bag. When ready to use, remove from the freezer and place in a bowl. Cover with a small tea towel and leave on the counter to thaw and rise.

This recipe can be easily doubled.

Add a drizzle of olive oil to the risen dough or to your fingertips to help spread it.

In a small bowl, combine the warm water, yeast, and sugar. Set aside to rise for 5 minutes.

In a large bowl, combine 1 cup of the flour, sea salt, onion powder, garlic powder, Italian seasoning, and oil.

Add the yeast to the flour mixture while stirring. When the dough becomes sticky, sprinkle in the remaining flour as required. Knead into a ball. Cover and let rest in a warm place for 20 to 30 minutes.

Preheat oven to 350°F.

Grease a pizza pan with butter or oil. Place the dough on the pan and spread by using your fingers to pull and shape the dough into a round. Spread sauce and add toppings.

Bake 30 minutes, checking the bottom of the crust for doneness.

PUMPERNICKEL BREAD

Makes 2 loaves

4⅓ cups multigrain flour

½ cup cornmeal

¼ cup cocoa

1 tbsp sea salt

2 cups milk (or 1 cup water, 1 cup milk)

1½ tbsp dark brown sugar

1 tbsp traditional or fast-rising yeast

¼ cup all-purpose white flour

¼ cup molasses

3 tbsp unsalted melted butter

BONITA'S TIPS
Do not deflate the dough before cutting it into pieces for the pans.

Bring the pans to room temperature or warmer before adding the dough.

Oil your hands before rolling the dough for best results.

In a large bowl, combine the multigrain flour, cornmeal, cocoa, and sea salt.

Heat ¾ cup of the milk in a medium bowl in the microwave for 20 to 30 seconds. Stir in the brown sugar and yeast. Let stand at room temperature for about 5 minutes to activate.

Stir the molasses and remaining milk into the yeast mixture, then add to the dry ingredients. Mix with a wooden spoon about 3 to 6 minutes, until the dough begins to pull away from the side of the bowl.

Add the melted butter. Mix until the butter is combined, about 3 minutes more. The dough will look greasy.

Knead the dough, adding the all-purpose white flour as you go, for about 3 to 5 minutes or until the dough is smooth and elastic. Form into a ball. Cut a cross in the top of the dough about ½ inch deep.

Cover the dough with parchment paper and a tea towel. Let rise at room temperature for 30 to 45 minutes. Lightly butter 2 loaf pans.

Do not deflate the dough. Cut in half. Cut each half into 3 pieces, rolling each inward into a ball and placing 3 balls into each loaf pan. Alternatively, form each half into a single round and place in a pie pan.

Cover with parchment paper and a tea towel and let rise in a warm place for 30 to 45 minutes.

Preheat oven to 350°F.

Bake for 35 minutes or until the crust is dark brown.

Remove from the pans and place on a cooling rack. Brush melted butter over the tops. Cover with parchment paper and a tea towel for 10 minutes to soften.

SALMON BREAD ROLLS

Makes 12 rolls

Filling

1 pound salmon, or more

1 tsp sea salt

8 oz cream cheese

2 tbsp sour cream

2 tbsp mayonnaise

¼ tsp white pepper

1 tsp onion powder

½ tsp dried or 1 tbsp fresh dill

1 tsp lemon juice

1 tbsp chopped green onion

Dough

2¼ cups all-purpose white flour

½ tsp sea salt

2 tsp fast-rising or traditional yeast

1 cup warm water

1 tsp sugar

1 large egg

1 tbsp melted butter

BONITA'S TIPS
If the yeast mixture does not bubble and rise after 5 minutes, discard and start again.

Make filling: Place salmon in a saucepan and cover with water. Add ½ teaspoon sea salt. Bring to a boil and simmer for about 5 minutes. Remove the salmon and place on a plate to cool.

Flake the salmon and place in a large bowl or food processor, reserve a few pieces to flake over the filling. Add all other ingredients except the green onion. Mix thoroughly.

Make dough: Combine 2 cups of the flour and sea salt in a large bowl.

Combine the warm water, yeast, and sugar in a small bowl. Let stand 5 minutes to activate.

Lightly beat the egg. Add to the dry ingredients. Stir in the melted butter. Pour in the yeast mixture. Mix with a wooden spoon or a stand mixer. When the dough becomes difficult to mix with the spoon, knead by hand for 5 to 10 minutes. Add small amounts of warm water or up to ¼ cup flour as required to make a smooth, elastic ball. Let rise 20 minutes in the bowl.

Assemble salmon roll: Roll the dough into a 12 x 10-inch rectangle, about ½ inch thick. Spread the salmon-cream cheese filling evenly over the dough. Top with more cooked salmon and sprinkle with green onions.

Roll the dough carefully away from you into a uniform log. Cut into 1-inch pieces. Grease or line a 9 x 13-inch baking pan with parchment paper and place the rolls evenly in the pan, cut side up. Brush the tops with melted butter.

Preheat oven to 350°F.

Cover the rolls with a tea towel and let rise 15 to 20 minutes.

Bake 30 to 35 minutes or until golden and baked through. Brush with more melted butter and serve.

TOUTONS

Makes 15 toutons

4 cups all-purpose white flour

½ tsp sea salt

1 tbsp fast-rising or traditional yeast

1½ cups warm water

1 tsp white sugar

1 tbsp melted butter

Combine the flour and sea salt in a large bowl.

In a small bowl, combine the yeast, warm water, and sugar. Set aside to rise for 5 minutes.

Using a wooden spoon, make a hole in the flour mixture; pour in the yeast mixture and melted butter. Mix all ingredients using the spoon or a stand mixer. Add additional flour as required to pull the dough together. Add additional warm water if required.

Knead the dough until smooth, elastic, and no longer sticky. You should be able to hear the dough cracking as you fold it. Work the dough into a ball.

Sprinkle additional flour over the dough. Cover with parchment paper and a tea towel and set the dough in a warm place to rise for 30 minutes.

Do not deflate the dough. Cut the dough into pieces about half the size of your hand and flatten.

Preheat a frying pan over medium heat. Add 1 tablespoon butter and 1 tablespoon olive oil. Place 3 to 4 pieces of dough in the pan; fry 4 to 5 minutes on each side until golden brown.

GLUTEN-FREE TOUTONS

Makes 6 toutons

1½ cups gluten-free
all-purpose white flour

1½ tbsp white sugar

½ tsp sea salt

1 tsp xanthan gum

1 tsp fast-rising or
traditional yeast

½ cup warm water

¼ cup warmed milk

2 tbsp melted butter

1 large egg

In a large bowl, mix the flour, 1 tablespoon sugar, sea salt, and xanthan gum.

In a small bowl, combine the yeast, warm water, and ½ tablespoon sugar. Let stand for 5 minutes to activate.

Add the yeast mixture to the flour. Beat using a wooden spoon, hand mixer, or stand mixer. Continue to beat while adding the warm milk and melted butter. Combine thoroughly.

Beat in the egg. Scrape the sides and bottom of the bowl, then beat at high speed for 3 minutes or so to make a very smooth and thick batter. Use more flour or warm water if needed.

Cover the bowl, and let the batter rise for 45 minutes to 1 hour in a warm place. **Do not deflate**. Scoop out the batter and shape into toutons and fry as above.

BONITA'S TIPS
Gluten-free touton dough can be used in a waffle iron or frying pan, and leftovers can be kept in the refrigerator for a day but should not be frozen.

It is a good habit to crack eggs into a small bowl to check for shells or spots before adding to other ingredients.

SWEET DOUGH

CHRISTMAS FRUIT BREAD

Makes 1 bread wreath and 2 loaves

1 cup warm water

2 tbsp fast-rising or traditional yeast

¾ cup + 1 tbsp white sugar

7 to 8 cups all-purpose white flour

½ tsp sea salt

2 cups mixed dried fruit/peel

½ cup unsalted melted butter

2 cups warm milk

2 eggs

1 tbsp vanilla

In a small bowl, combine the warm water, yeast, and 1 tablespoon of the sugar. Set aside to rise for 5 minutes.

Sift 7 cups of the flour into a large bowl. Add ¾ cup sugar, sea salt, and mixed fruit/peel. Make a hole in the middle of the mixture.

In a second bowl, combine the melted butter, warm milk, eggs, and vanilla. Pour into the hole in the flour mixture. Pour in the risen yeast and mix with a wooden spoon until everything comes together. Use up to 1 cup of additional flour if required.

When the mixture is too stiff to move with the wooden spoon, work the dough with your hand, leaving one hand on the bowl and using one for the dough. Pull the dough toward you and push it down into the bowl, adding extra flour as needed.

When the dough has formed a ball, flip it over. Cut a ½-inch-deep cross into the top of the dough with a knife, cover with a lid or parchment paper and a tea towel, and place in a warm area to rise.

Let rise for about 30 minutes, until the dough is half the size again. Knead briefly to deflate, then form the dough into a ball again. Cover and let rise another 30 minutes.

Grease 2 loaf pans and a Bundt pan (for a wreath), or 3 loaf pans. Cut the dough into 9 pieces. Form 6 pieces into balls, and place them in the pans—3 balls in each pan.

To make a wreath, roll each of the remaining pieces of dough into a 20-inch-long dough log. Pinch the 3 pieces together at the top, braid, and lay in the Bundt pan.

Cover the pans with a tea towel and let rise for 30 to 40 minutes, or until the dough has increased again by half.

Preheat oven to 350°F. Bake for 35 minutes or until golden brown. Glaze with butter, then place parchment paper and a tea towel over the cooling bread to soften.

CINNAMON BLUEBERRY STICKY ROLLS

Makes 12 large rolls

Dough

1 tbsp fast-rising or traditional yeast

¼ cup warm water

3½ cups all-purpose white flour

¼ cup white sugar

Pinch sea salt

3 tbsp melted butter

1¼ cups warmed milk

2 large eggs, lightly beaten

2 tsp vanilla

In a small bowl, combine the warm water, yeast, and a pinch of white sugar. Set aside to rise for 5 minutes.

In a large bowl, combine 2 cups of the flour with the remaining white sugar and sea salt. Mix in the melted butter, warm milk, vanilla, and eggs. Add the yeast mixture. Using a wooden spoon or a stand mixer, stir for about 5 minutes or until the dough has no lumps and the mixture starts to get sticky.

Using one hand to turn the bowl and the other to fold the dough toward you, fold the dough continuously. Add and incorporate 1 cup of flour (more if needed) to help form a ball.

Cover dough with parchment paper and a tea towel. Set aside to rise for 1 hour.

Sticky glaze for pan

½ cup melted butter

1 cup brown sugar

Sticky filling

1 cup brown sugar

½ cup butter,
room temperature

3 tbsp cinnamon

2½ cups fresh or frozen
blueberries

Topping glaze

2 tbsp milk

1 tsp vanilla

1 cup icing sugar

1 tsp cinnamon

Then knead the dough, adding up to ¼ cup flour to help form a ball. The dough should feel spongy and make a cracking sound as you knead. After kneading, set aside for 10 minutes.

Dust the counter with ¼ cup of flour. Roll out the dough to about 1 inch thick. Grease a 9 x 13-inch pan or line with parchment paper.

Make sticky glaze: In a small bowl, mix the melted butter and brown sugar. Pour evenly into the pan.

Make sticky filling: Combine the brown sugar with the butter and cinnamon. Mix in the blueberries. Spread the filling evenly over the dough.

Roll the dough away from you into a log shape. Cut into 12 pieces and place on top of the sticky filling. Cover with parchment paper. Set aside and allow to rise until the rolls are half as large again.

Preheat oven to 350°F. Bake for 30 minutes or until the rolls are golden brown.

Make topping glaze: In a small bowl, combine the glaze ingredients. Pour over the rolls while they are still warm.

Serve hot or cold—these are amazing.

HOT CROSS BUNS

Makes 12 buns

2 tsp fast-rising or traditional yeast

¼ cup warm water

⅓ cup white sugar

3 cups all-purpose white flour

½ tsp sea salt

1 tbsp allspice (mixture of cinnamon, cloves, nutmeg, ginger)

1 cup mixed dried fruit

¼ cup melted butter

¾ cup warmed milk

2 large eggs

1 tbsp honey (for glazing after baking)

Paste for crosses
4 tbsp all-purpose white flour

3 tbsp water

In a small bowl, combine the warm water, yeast, and 1 teaspoon of the sugar. Set aside to rise for 5 minutes.

In a large bowl, combine 2 cups of the flour, the remaining sugar, salt, allspice, and dried fruit. Lightly beat the eggs and add to the dry ingredients, mixing with a wooden spoon or a stand mixer. Continue to mix as you add the melted butter, warm milk, and yeast.

When the dough starts to come together, use your hand to continue mixing and kneading. Add up to 1 additional cup flour to form the dough into a smooth ball. Cover the dough with plastic wrap and set in a warm place for 20 to 30 minutes to rise.

Make the paste for the crosses by mixing the flour and water.

Cut the risen dough into 12 small pieces. Roll each piece by hand outward and under into a ball, then place in a 9-inch square baking pan.

Cut a cross on the top of each bun. Pour the paste into a plastic sandwich bag, cut off one corner, and draw a cross over each bun. Put the buns in a warm area to rise for 20 to 30 minutes. Preheat oven to 350°F.

Bake for 20 to 25 minutes. Remove from the oven and glaze with the honey immediately with a pastry brush.

Enjoy with butter or jam.

Partridgeberry
Muffins

QUICK BREADS, SCONES, AND MUFFINS

BANANA ALMOND SPICE BREAD

Makes 1 loaf or 12 muffins

½ cup brown sugar

½ cup salted butter

2 to 3 medium bananas
(frozen or overripe),
mashed

2 eggs, lightly beaten

2 cups all-purpose
white flour

1 tsp baking powder

1 tsp baking soda

1 tsp ground cloves

1 tsp ground cinnamon

¼ cup orange juice

1 tsp vanilla

½ cup crushed or
chopped almonds

Preheat oven to 350°F.

Cream the sugar and butter in a medium bowl. Add the bananas and eggs and mix thoroughly.

Sift together the dry ingredients and fold into the banana mixture. Add the orange juice and vanilla. Fold in the almonds.

Pour the batter into a greased loaf pan or muffin pans.

Bake for 40 to 60 minutes or until golden brown. Check by inserting a knife into the centre of the bread—if the knife comes out clean, it is done. If the knife is covered in batter, return the bread to the oven for a few more minutes.

BONITA'S TIPS

Line the loaf pan with parchment paper to prevent the loaf from burning.

Serve warm with butter, whipped cream, or berries, or combine cream cheese and icing sugar and spread over the bread.

BLUEBERRY SCONES
WITH **LEMON GLAZE**

Makes 12 or 24 scones

2¾ cups all-purpose white flour

½ cup white sugar

1 tbsp baking powder

¼ tsp baking soda

¼ tsp sea salt

1 cup cold butter

1 cup evaporated milk

½ cup fresh or frozen blueberries

2 tbsp freshly squeezed lemon juice

Zest of 1 lemon

Lemon glaze

2 tsp lemon juice

2 tsp lemon zest (optional)

4 to 6 tbsp icing sugar

BONITA'S TIPS

If you are using frozen blueberries, there is no need to thaw.

Over-mixing the blueberries squeezes the juice out of the berries (and you end up with blue batter!).

Preheat oven to 350°F.

Reserve ¼ cup of the flour to toss with the blueberries. Sift the remaining dry ingredients into a large bowl. Cut the butter into ¼-inch cubes and work into the dry ingredients using your hand or a stand mixer.

Combine the milk, lemon juice, and zest in a small bowl. Pour over the flour-butter mixture and mix until the ingredients come together into a ball. Toss the blueberries in the remaining flour and fold gently into the batter.

Sprinkle the counter or pastry board with flour. Gently roll or press the dough into a circle; try to avoid cracking the blueberries.

Cover a cookie sheet with parchment paper. Cut the dough circle into 12 medium wedges or 24 small wedges, separate, and place the wedges on the cookie sheet.

Bake for 20 minutes or until golden brown. Remove from the oven and drizzle with the lemon glaze.

Lemon glaze: In a small bowl, combine all ingredients. Pour equal amounts of lemon glaze over cold or warm blueberry scones.

DATE NUT LOAF

Makes 1 loaf

1 cup water

2 cups pitted dates, chopped

1 cup brown sugar

½ cup butter

1 tsp cloves or allspice

2 cups all-purpose white flour

1 tsp sea salt

1 tsp baking powder

½ cup crushed or chopped nuts (assortment or nuts of choice)

¼ cup cold water

1 tsp baking soda

Preheat oven to 400°F.

Add 1 cup water to a medium saucepan and bring to a boil. Add the dates, brown sugar, butter, and spice. Remove from the heat and let sit 10 to 15 minutes.

In a large bowl, sift together the flour, sea salt, and baking powder.

Add the baking soda to the cold water and add to the date mixture. Pour the mixture into the dry ingredients and fold together slowly until combined. Fold in the nuts.

Pour the batter into a greased loaf pan or a Bundt pan. Bake for 45 minutes to 1 hour, until a knife inserted in the centre comes out clean.

BONITA'S TIPS
Sifting lightens the flour and results in a cakelike batter.

HARD BREAD (HARD TACK)

Makes 12 biscuits

When prepared properly, this will look, feel, and taste exactly like store-bought hard bread.

5 cups all-purpose white flour

1½ cups water

1 tbsp sea salt

Preheat oven to 425°F.

Mix the ingredients in a large bowl. Add more water if needed. Knead and pat or roll out into a rectangle about 1½ inches thick.

Cut into 12 squares. Use a knife to poke 6 little holes in the top of each. Place the dough on an ungreased cookie sheet.

Bake 40 to 60 minutes or until golden brown and the dough becomes hard.

GLUTEN-FREE HARD BREAD

Makes 3 biscuits

1 cup gluten-free
all-purpose white flour

½ tsp xanthan gum

⅓ cup water

1 tsp sea salt

Preheat oven to 425°F.

In a medium bowl, combine all ingredients with a fork. Knead together, using one hand to fold dough inward until the mixture comes together.

Dust the counter with additional gluten-free flour and roll the dough into a 7 x 4-inch rectangle about ½ inch thick. Cut into 3 equal biscuits. Place on an ungreased cookie sheet. Bake for 50 minutes or until dry and golden brown.

Remove from the oven and cool on a cooling rack.

BONITA'S TIPS

Do not add too much water to hard bread dough—this is a low hydration bread.

Store hard bread in a paper bag in a dry cupboard, or in a freezer bag in the freezer.

When ready to use, soak the hard bread overnight in cold water to soften.

Warm in a saucepan on low heat for 5 minutes. Serve with cooked salted cod or on its own.

MOLASSES BUNS

Makes 12 medium or 24 small buns

½ cup molasses

½ cup boiling water

1½ tsp baking soda

½ cup brown sugar

½ cup butter,
room temperature

1 tbsp allspice

1 tbsp ginger

1 tbsp cinnamon

3 cups all-purpose
white flour

1 large egg

1 tbsp milk

½ tsp sea salt

½ cup pork fat pieces
(optional)

Preheat oven to 350°F.

In a large bowl, mix the molasses, boiling water, and baking soda with a spoon until it fizzes. Add the brown sugar, butter, and spices, and stir.

In a small bowl, whisk the egg and milk. Add to the molasses mixture and stir to combine.

Sift the flour and sea salt into the mixture and stir; use your hands to fold the ingredients together, if required. Dust with more flour if the mixture is too soft. Shape into a ball, cover with plastic wrap, and place in the refrigerator for 1 hour.

Sprinkle additional flour on the counter or pastry board. Cut the dough in half. Add optional pork fat pieces and roll half the dough out to about 1½ inch thick. Use a 3-inch round cookie cutter or glass to cut the buns. Alternatively, instead of rolling, pinch off pieces of dough and pat to the desired size. Place the dough on parchment paper on a cookie sheet. Continue with the second half of the dough.

Bake for 15 minutes.

BONITA'S TIPS
The butter can be replaced by pork fat. To do so, fry small pieces of fat pork and drain off the fat. Use ½ cup to replace the butter in this recipe. You can use pork scrunchions instead of pork fat pieces.

PARTRIDGEBERRY MUFFINS

Makes 12 muffins

1 cup butter,
room temperature

1 cup white sugar

2 large eggs

1 cup milk

1 tsp vanilla

2 cups all-purpose
white flour

½ tsp sea salt

2 tsp baking powder

1 cup fresh or frozen
partridgeberries

Preheat oven to 400°F.

Cream the butter and sugar until fluffy.

In a separate bowl, whisk the eggs, milk, and vanilla. Mix into the butter and sugar.

Sift 1½ cups of the flour, sea salt, and baking powder. Add the wet ingredients and stir just to combine.

Toss the partridgeberries with ½ cup of the flour until coated. Fold the berries into the batter.

Grease or line muffin pans. Scoop equal amounts of the batter into each one, filling about ¾ full.

Bake 25 minutes or until golden brown.

BONITA'S TIPS
Double-sift flour to give the muffins a cakelike texture.

Place baked muffins on a cooling rack. Cover with a tea towel for 5 minutes, then remove the towel and sift icing sugar over the tops of the muffins.

PUMPKIN CARROT WALNUT MUFFINS WITH **CREAM CHEESE FROSTING**

Makes 12 muffins

½ cup butter

¾ cup brown sugar

2 large eggs

½ cup maple syrup

1 cup pumpkin filling
(see recipe page 78
or use tinned)

1½ cups shredded carrots

2½ cups all-purpose
white flour

1½ tsp baking powder

1 tsp baking soda

½ tsp sea salt

2 or 3 tsp pumpkin pie spice

1 cup chopped walnuts

Cream cheese frosting

8 oz cream cheese

½ cup butter

½ cup brown sugar

1 tbsp maple syrup

1 tbsp pumpkin filling

½ tsp pumpkin pie spice

2 cups icing sugar

BONITA'S TIPS
Fill muffin cups only
¾ full.

Preheat oven to 350°F.

In a large bowl, cream the butter and brown sugar.

In a small bowl, lightly beat the eggs. Add the maple syrup and pumpkin filling and combine. Fold into the butter and brown sugar. Stir in the shredded carrots.

Sift the flour, baking powder, baking soda, sea salt, and pumpkin pie spice into the batter. Fold in the walnuts.

Grease or line the muffin pan. Scoop equal amounts of the batter into each muffin cup.

Bake 30 to 35 minutes or until a toothpick inserted in the centre comes out clean. Cool completely before icing.

Cream cheese frosting: Beat the cream cheese and butter. Continue beating while adding the brown sugar, maple syrup, pumpkin filling, pumpkin pie spice, and icing sugar. Beat until smooth and thick.

SODA BREAD

Make 4 buns or 1 loaf

4 cups all-purpose white flour

2 tbsp white sugar

1 tsp sea salt

1 tsp baking soda

4 tbsp cold butter

1 cup raisins (optional)

1 large egg, lightly beaten

1¾ cups evaporated milk or whole milk

1 tsp vanilla

Preheat oven to 375°F.

Combine the dry ingredients, including the raisins.

Cut the butter into small cubes. Add to the dry ingredients and work in by pinching with your hand or using a potato masher.

Make a hole in the middle of the mixture and add the milk, vanilla, and lightly beaten egg. Mix with a wooden spoon and then knead by hand.

Dust the counter with additional flour and set the dough on top. Either cut the dough into 4 pieces and shape into balls, or shape the dough into one round loaf.

Place the balls in a greased 9-inch square pan or the round loaf on parchment paper on a baking sheet. Bake 20 to 30 minutes or until golden brown.

BONITA'S TIPS

Use parchment paper to line the bottom of the pan for easy removal and to help prevent burning.

Put a dab of butter in each corner of the pan under the parchment paper to keep the paper from lifting.

Serve soda bread with soup or jam and butter.

Lemon Crumbles

COOKIES AND SQUARES

APPLE SQUARES WITH TOFFEE SAUCE

Makes 12 squares

1 or 2 bottles of
sweet apple wedges
(see recipe below)

4 cups graham cracker
crumbs

½ cup melted butter

¼ cup brown or
white sugar

1 envelope (15 ml) gelatin

¼ cup cold water

1 cup whipping cream

1 cup icing sugar

Toffee sauce
¼ cup brown sugar

2 tbsp salted butter

1 tbsp cream or milk

Preheat oven to 350°F.

Combine the crumbs, melted butter, and sugar in a large bowl.

Line an 8-inch square pan with parchment paper. Add the crumb mixture and pat down firmly. Bake for 15 minutes or until golden brown. Remove and let cool.

In a bowl, sprinkle the gelatin over the water. Let sit until jelled, about 5 minutes. Place the apple wedges and their liquid in a saucepan over medium heat.

When the gelatin has set, pour in 1 cup of the hot apple liquid and stir. Fold in the apple wedges. Place the bowl in the refrigerator until the liquid starts to gel (this will take about 1 hour).

Pour the whipping cream into a medium bowl and beat in the icing sugar. Continue beating until stiff peaks form.

Spoon the chilled apple filling over the crust, then top with the whipped cream.

Refrigerate for at least 2 hours or overnight. Cut into squares and serve with toffee sauce.

Toffee sauce: Place all ingredients in a small bowl and heat in the microwave until the butter melts (about 30 seconds to 1 minute). Remove from the microwave and stir with a fork or whisk to blend into a thick sauce.

SWEET APPLE WEDGES

Makes 3 x 500 ml bottles

6 to 8 apples of choice

½ tsp lemon juice

5 cups water

½ tsp sea salt

1 cup apple juice

1 cup brown sugar

1 tsp cinnamon

⅛ tsp nutmeg

Peel the apples and cut into wedges. Place the wedges in a bowl and coat with the lemon juice. Let rest 5 minutes.

Fill a large saucepan halfway with about 4 cups of the water, add the sea salt, and bring to a boil. Carefully add the apple wedges and boil 5 minutes. Drain the water, leaving the apple wedges in the saucepan to keep warm until ready to use.

In another saucepan, combine 1 cup of the water, the apple juice, brown sugar, cinnamon, and nutmeg and bring to a boil. Boil 5 minutes.

Sterilize three 500 ml Mason jars. Divide the apple wedges between the bottles and pour equal amounts of the juice mixture into each one. Clean the rims and place the lids and caps on tightly. Process in a water bath for 5 to 10 minutes. *Please follow proper canning methods to sterilize and seal jars.*

Please Note: *This is not a pie filling, but it can become one!* To fill a pie, remove the apples and liquid from the bottle and heat in a saucepan. Use cornstarch to thicken the liquid before pouring the apples into pie crusts. Add more spices to taste.

APRICOT SQUARES

Makes 24 squares

Filling

24 fresh apricots

1 cup white sugar

1 tsp lemon zest

½ tsp lemon juice

Crust

½ cup butter

½ to 1 cup white sugar

2 cups all-purpose white flour

½ tsp sea salt

3 tsp baking powder

½ cup evaporated milk

BONITA'S TIPS

Let the dough cool in the refrigerator for 5 to 10 minutes to harden the butter before rolling.

Make the filling a day in advance (or at least a few hours ahead) to give it time to cool completely before using.

If fresh apricots are unavailable, use 4 cups frozen or dried apricots, following the same method.

Make filling: Clean the apricots, remove their stones, and cut into pieces. In a small saucepan, combine the apricots and sugar. Cook over a low heat until the mixture starts to condense and thicken, about 5 to 10 minutes. Remove from the heat. Add the lemon zest and lemon and stir to combine. Let cool completely.

Preheat oven to 350°F.

Make crust: In a large bowl, cream the butter and sugar. Sift in the flour, sea salt, and baking powder. Slowly add milk to the mixture until thoroughly combined. Form the dough into a ball and knead by hand or by a stand mixer. Add 1 to 2 tablespoons or two of additional milk if required. Cut the dough in half.

On parchment paper or flour-dusted counter, roll half of the dough into a 9-inch square about ¼ inch thick. Place the dough on a cookie sheet.

Spread the filling over the dough. Roll out the second half of the dough. Place on top of the filling.

Bake for 20 minutes or until light golden brown.

Remove from the oven and let cool. Cut into squares or bars. Serve with a cup of tea.

GINGERBREAD HOUSE
OR COOKIES

1 house or 12 cookies

¾ cup soft butter

1 cup brown sugar

2 tsp ground ginger

1 tsp cinnamon

1 tsp cloves

½ cup molasses

1 tsp baking soda

2½ cups all-purpose
white or whole wheat flour

In a large bowl, cream the butter, brown sugar, and spices.

In a small bowl, combine the molasses and baking soda; pour into the butter mixture and stir to make a smooth batter.

Sift the flour gradually into the batter, mixing with a wooden spoon. Add up to 1 tablespoon water if needed. When the cookie mixture starts to form a ball, continue working in the flour with your hand.

When the dough comes together into a ball, cover with plastic wrap and refrigerate for 2 hours.

Icing for gingerbread house

5 cups icing sugar

½ tsp cream of tartar

7 tbsp water

1 tsp almond or mint extract

1 tsp corn syrup

½ tsp sea salt

Preheat oven to 350°F. Roll the dough to ⅛ inch thick. Cut out the gingerbread house pieces (see instructions below) or cookies. Place on parchment paper-lined cookie sheets. Bake 10 to 12 minutes.

GINGERBREAD HOUSE: After rolling out the dough, cut 4 rectangles measuring 3 x 5 inches each (these will be two side walls and the roof). Cut 2 squares measuring 5 x 5 inches (the back and front walls); mark and cut a peak from the 3-inch mark. Bake and cool.

Place the side walls on a plate, cutting board, or other base. Run a line of icing on the outer edges of the wall pieces and use the icing to stick the end walls in place. Run more icing along the edges so that all four walls are joined firmly together. Affix the roof with icing. Support the outside walls so that they do not fall down while waiting for the structural icing to harden.

Decorate the house as you wish.

ICING FOR GINGERBREAD HOUSE: Combine all ingredients and mix until blended; add extra icing sugar if needed. Cover the bowl with plastic wrap and place in the refrigerator until ready to use. Use a decorating bag to ice the gingerbread house. Add food colouring to some of the icing if desired. This icing will form a hard, edible mortar to keep your gingerbread house together.

BONITA'S TIPS
See video at www.bonitaskitchen.com for more instructions.

LEMON CRUMBLES

Makes 16 or 20 squares

2 cups all-purpose white flour

1 tsp baking powder

¾ cup white sugar

2 cups unsweetened shredded coconut

1 cup melted butter

Filling

½ cup lemon juice

1 14-oz can sweetened condensed milk

1 tsp lemon zest (optional)

Preheat oven to 350°F.

Combine the flour, baking powder, sugar, and coconut in a medium bowl. Add the melted butter and mix thoroughly.

In a separate bowl, whisk the filling ingredients until smooth and thickened.

Line a 9-inch square pan with parchment paper and press half the crumble mixture into the bottom of the pan. Cover evenly with the lemon filling. Top with the remaining crumble but do not press down.

Bake for 30 minutes. Do not overbake.

Let cool in the pan. Remove the crumble by pulling the parchment paper up from each side. Use a sharp knife to cut into 2-inch squares.

BONITA'S TIPS

You can use a stand mixer to make the crumble but only to pulse together—do not process into a ball.

Sweetened condensed milk is thick; place the can in warm water before opening to help it pour or use a spatula to scoop it out.

OATMEAL RAISIN COOKIES

Makes 24 cookies

2 cups oatmeal

1 cup brown sugar

2 tsp baking powder

½ cup melted butter

1 large egg

½ tsp vanilla

1 cup raisins

Preheat oven to 350°F.

Combine the oatmeal, brown sugar, and baking powder in a medium bowl. Add the melted butter and fold together.

In a small bowl, beat the egg and vanilla. Pour into the oatmeal mixture and combine thoroughly. Stir in the raisins.

Line a cookie sheet with parchment paper. Drop the batter by half-tablespoons about 3 inches apart.

Bake 8 to 10 minutes. Let cool for a few minutes before removing the cookies from the pan.

**Carrot Cake with
Cream Cheese Icing**

CAKES

CARROT CAKE WITH CREAM CHEESE ICING

Makes one 2-layer cake

½ cup butter

1 cup white sugar

3 cups grated carrots

1 tsp vanilla

½ cup applesauce

1 cup crushed pineapple, drained

1½ cups chopped walnuts or pecans (+ extra for garnish)

4 large eggs

2 cups all-purpose white flour

1 tsp sea salt

1 tsp cinnamon

2 tsp baking soda

1 tsp baking powder

Cream cheese icing

8 oz cream cheese, room temperature

½ cup butter, room temperature

1 tsp vanilla

3½ cups icing sugar

Cream Cheese Frosting (recipe below)

Preheat oven to 350°F.

In a medium bowl, cream the butter and sugar. Add the grated carrots and vanilla and combine. Add the applesauce, crushed pineapple, and 1 cup of the nuts, and fold together.

Mix in the eggs, one at a time. Sift in the flour, sea salt, cinnamon, baking powder, and baking soda and combine.

Grease two 9-inch round cake pans. Spread the batter in the pans. Bake 40 to 60 minutes; check for doneness with a toothpick or knife. Let the pan cool on a cooling rack before removing the cake.

Ice cake with cream cheese frosting; garnish with chopped nuts.

Cream cheese icing: In a medium bowl, beat the cream cheese and butter. Add the vanilla. Slowly beat in the icing sugar.

DARK RUM FRUIT CAKE

Makes 1 small cake or loaf

¼ cup chopped red cherries

¼ cup chopped green cherries

¼ cup chopped pitted dates

¼ cup mixed dried fruit

¼ cup chopped dried cranberries

½ cup dark rum (or more)

½ cup butter

¼ cup brown sugar

1 large egg

1 cup all-purpose white flour

¼ tsp baking soda

½ tsp ground cinnamon

¼ tsp sea salt

¼ cup dark molasses

2 tbsp milk

1 tsp allspice or cloves

BONITA'S TIPS
Write the date you made the cake on the container. If you are eager, this cake can be eaten after 11 days. If you cannot wait 11 days, just re-open the container and enjoy.

In a medium bowl with a lid, combine all the fruit and ¼ cup of the rum. Cover and soak at least a few hours or overnight at room temperature.

Preheat oven to 325°F.

In a large bowl, cream the butter and brown sugar. Add the egg and mix thoroughly. In another bowl, sift the flour, baking soda, cinnamon, allspice, and sea salt. In a third bowl, combine the molasses and milk.

Alternate adding the flour mixture and the molasses mixture to the butter mixture, while stirring, until well incorporated. Fold the rum and fruit mixture into the batter.

Line a 6 x 3-inch springform pan with parchment paper and oil around the inside. Scoop the batter into the pan and bake for 45 minutes. Test by poking a toothpick or knife into the cake: if it comes out clean, the cake is ready; if it is not, bake 5 minutes more and test again.

Let the cake cool for 10 minutes in the pan, then remove the cake and place on a cooling rack. When completely cool, sprinkle 1 tablespoon dark rum over the top.

Soak a piece of cheesecloth in ¼ cup of the dark rum. Wrap the cheesecloth around the cake, then wrap with parchment paper.

Place the cake in an airtight container with a lid and store for 10 weeks in a cool place or in the refrigerator.

DOUBLE CHOCOLATE CAKE

Makes 1 cake

½ cup butter

½ cup brown sugar

1 tsp vanilla

½ tsp sea salt

¼ cup freshly brewed coffee
(or ½ tsp instant coffee
granules dissolved in
¼ cup warm water)

2 large eggs, lightly beaten

¾ cup milk

2 cups all-purpose
white flour

4 tbsp cocoa

2 tsp baking powder

½ tsp nutmeg

½ tsp cinnamon

½ cup unsweetened
chocolate chips

Chocolate icing
250 ml whipping cream

1 cup icing sugar

2 tbsp cocoa

Chocolate topping
1 cup semi-sweet
chocolate chips

1 tbsp milk

1 tsp vanilla

Preheat oven to 350°F.

Cream the butter, sugar, and vanilla in a large bowl. Add the eggs, milk, and coffee, and combine thoroughly.

Sift the dry ingredients into a separate bowl. Add to the liquid ingredients and combine. Fold in the chocolate chips.

Grease a 9-inch square pan or a round springform pan or line the pan with parchment paper. Add the batter.

Bake for 30 minutes or until a knife inserted in the batter comes out clean. Let the baked cake rest for 10 minutes, then remove from the pan and cool on a cooling rack.

Chocolate icing: Whip the cream until stiff peaks form using a hand mixer. Add the cocoa and icing sugar and mix well. Add more icing sugar if needed to reach the desired consistency. Refrigerate until ready to use.

Chocolate topping: Melt the chocolate chips in the microwave or double boiler, stirring often until melted. Stir in the milk and vanilla. Spoon the chocolate over the baked and iced cake. Place the cake in the refrigerator or a cool room to set.

POUND CAKE WITH COCONUT BUTTER ICING

Makes 1 cake

¾ cup butter,
room temperature

¾ cup white sugar

3 large eggs

1 tsp vanilla

¼ cup milk

1½ cups all-purpose
white flour

1½ tsp baking powder

½ tsp sea salt

Preheat oven to 350°F.

In a large bowl, cream the butter and sugar using a wooden spoon or a hand mixer. Continue to mix while adding the eggs, one at a time, vanilla, and milk.

Double-sift the flour, baking powder, and sea salt and add to the wet ingredients. Combine thoroughly.

Bake 45 to 60 minutes or until a toothpick inserted in the middle of the cake comes out clean.

Cool the cake on a cooling rack. Ice with coconut butter icing.

Coconut butter icing

½ cup butter,
room temperature

1 tsp vanilla

1 tsp coconut oil

3 tbsp evaporated milk

3 cups icing sugar

½ cup unsweetened
shredded coconut

Coconut butter icing: In a small bowl, use a wooden spoon or a hand mixer to combine the butter, vanilla, coconut oil, and milk.

Slowly mix in the icing sugar until smooth and creamy. Fold in the coconut.

Let set in the refrigerator before using.

BONITA'S TIPS
Store leftover icing in a Mason jar with a lid in the refrigerator.

TOMATO SOUP CAKE
WITH **BUTTERCREAM ICING**

Makes 1 cake

¾ cup butter,
room temperature

1 cup brown sugar

1 284-ml can tomato soup

3 cups sifted all-purpose
white flour

1 tsp baking soda

2 tsp baking powder

2 cups raisins

½ cup chopped
glacé baking cherries

2 tsp allspice

Buttercream icing

½ cup butter

4 oz cream cheese

1 tbsp maple syrup

¼ cup brown sugar

1 cup icing sugar

1 tsp allspice

Preheat oven to 350°F.

In a medium bowl, cream the butter, sugar, and tomato soup until combined.

Sift 2¾ cups of the flour, baking soda, and baking powder. Mix into the butter mixture. Fill the tomato soup can with cold water and add to the batter. Stir.

Toss the cherries and raisins with ¼ cup of the flour and allspice. Fold into the batter.

Spoon the batter into a greased cake pan or a Bundt pan. Bake 55 to 60 minutes.

Remove from the oven; let rest 10 minutes before removing from the pan onto a cooling rack.

Ice with buttercream icing or serve with whipped cream.

Buttercream icing: Cream the butter and cream cheese. Add the maple syrup, brown sugar, icing sugar, and allspice. Continue mixing until smooth; add more icing sugar if needed.

BONITA'S TIPS
Toss the cherries and raisins in flour to keep them from falling to the bottom of the cake.

UPSIDE DOWN RHUBARB CAKE

Makes one 9-inch square cake

9 sticks fresh rhubarb, in 1-inch pieces

Brown sugar sauce
½ cup brown sugar

¼ cup orange juice

½ tsp lemon zest

Batter
1 cup butter, room temperature

¾ cup white sugar

3 large eggs

1 tsp vanilla

2 cups all-purpose white flour

1½ tsp baking powder

1 cup evaporated milk

½ tsp lemon juice

Make brown sugar sauce: In a small saucepan, combine the brown sugar and orange juice and bring to a boil for 2 to 3 minutes. Add the lemon zest. Turn down the heat and simmer for 2 minutes until the mixture is a thick syrup. Remove from the heat.

Make batter: Cream the butter and sugar. Add the eggs, one at a time, to the butter and sugar. Mix until light and fluffy. Stir in the vanilla.

In another bowl, sift the flour and baking powder. Fold the dry ingredients into the butter mixture. Do not over-mix. Add the milk and fold the ingredients together. Add the lemon juice and stir just to incorporate.

Assemble cake: Preheat oven to 350°F. Grease one 9-inch square or a 9 x 13-inch rectangular pan, or line with parchment paper. Arrange the rhubarb pieces on the bottom of the pan. Pour the syrup over the rhubarb. Spoon the batter over the top and smooth it. Bake 45 to 60 minutes. Insert a toothpick into the cake to check for doneness: if it comes out clean, the cake is ready; if it is wet, close the oven door and leave another 5 minutes.

Let the cake set in the pan for 5 to 10 minutes before inverting it onto a plate.

BONITA'S TIPS
Leave the rhubarb peels on if you wish to have more colour and form.

Run a knife around the sides of the cake before inverting.

Do not overbake!

Maple Butter Tarts

PIES AND PASTRIES

COCONUT CREAM PIE

Makes one 9-inch pie

½ cup butter

¾ cup white sugar

1 cup evaporated milk

3 large eggs

1 tsp vanilla

2 tbsp all-purpose white flour

1¼ cups unsweetened shredded coconut

Pinch sea salt

Preheat oven to 350°F.

Cream the butter and sugar. Add the milk, eggs, vanilla, and flour. Mix by wooden spoon, hand mixer, or stand mixer.

Fold in the coconut.

Pour the mixture into the unbaked pie crust. Bake for 45 to 50 minutes or until golden brown. Poke a toothpick in the pie; if it comes out clean, it is ready.

Remove from the oven and let cool.

**Unbaked pie crust
(recipe below)**

Cream

500 ml whipping cream

¼ cup icing sugar

1 tsp vanilla

To serve

1 cup unsweetened
shredded coconut

In a cold bowl, whip the cream with the icing sugar and salt using a hand mixer until fluffy. Spread over the top of the cooled pie.

Toast the 1 cup unsweetened coconut in a frying pan on medium heat until golden brown. Sprinkle over the pie before serving.

9-INCH PIE CRUST

Makes 2 crusts

½ cup cold butter

2 cups all-purpose white
or whole wheat flour

½ tsp sea salt

½ cup cold water

Preheat oven to 350°F.

Cut the butter into small cubes. Mix the flour, butter, and sea salt in a bowl by hand or using a food processor. Add the water and continue to mix just until the dough shapes into a ball.

Place parchment paper on the counter and sprinkle with additional flour. Cut the dough in half. Roll out half on the parchment paper. Place in a pie dish.

BONITA'S TIPS

If you are only using one pie crust, roll the other out on parchment paper, cover with plastic wrap, then roll into a cylinder. Freeze until needed.

KEY LIME PIE

Makes 1 pie

9-inch pie crust, baked
(see recipe, page 71)

4 eggs

½ cup freshly squeezed
key lime juice

½ cup white sugar

1 14-oz can sweetened
condensed milk

½ tsp cream of tartar

Make pie crust: Bake for 10 to 12 minutes at 350°F.

Make filling: Separate the eggs. Whisk egg yolks vigorously with a hand whisk until the yolks turn an opaque lemon colour. Pour in the condensed milk slowly and continue to mix until combined. Add the lime juice and mix. Place the bowl in the refrigerator.

Make meringue: Add the cream of tartar to the egg whites and beat until foamy. Add the sugar a little at a time, beating continuously until stiff peaks form.

Preheat oven to 350°F. Fold 6 tablespoons of the meringue into the lime filling. Pour into the prepared crust. Gently spread the remaining meringue on top.

Bake for 10 minutes or until golden brown. Remove and cool before cutting.

LEMON MERINGUE PIE

Makes one 9-inch pie

Filling

3 tbsp cornstarch

3 tbsp all-purpose white flour

1 cup white sugar

1 cup boiling water

4 tbsp lemon juice

Zest of 1 or 2 lemons

2 tsp butter

3 egg yolks

Meringue

3 egg whites, room temperature

1 cup white sugar

½ tsp cold water

9-inch pie crust, baked (see recipe, page 71)

Make pie crust: Bake for 10 to 12 minutes at 350°F. Remove from the oven, then increase the oven temperature to 400°F.

Make filling: In a large saucepan, combine the cornstarch, flour, and sugar. Place on medium heat and slowly add the boiling water while stirring. Cook for 2 minutes, then add the lemon juice, lemon zest, and butter, still stirring.

In a small bowl, lightly whisk the egg yolks. Slowly add ⅓ cup of the hot lemon liquid to the egg yolks while whisking. Pour the yolk mixture into the saucepan and continue whisking. When thoroughly mixed, remove the saucepan from the heat and set aside.

BONITA'S TIPS

Be sure to add **hot** water to the saucepan while whisking the filling.

Make the pastry with cold butter and put the pastry in the refrigerator after forming a ball to cool before rolling out.

Be sure to let the pie cool completely before serving; if you try to cut it while it is still warm, it will fall apart.

Make meringue: Pour the room-temperature egg whites into a small glass bowl and use a high-speed mixer to whip. When soft peaks start to form, add ½ tsp cold water. Slowly add the sugar; continue mixing until all the sugar is resolved and stiff peaks have formed.

Pour the lemon filling into the baked pie crust. Top with the meringue and bake until golden brown.

Let cool on the counter. Refrigerate until ready to serve.

MAPLE BUTTER TARTS

Makes 12 to 16 tarts

1 cup raisins

½ cup maple syrup

1 cup brown sugar

¼ cup unsalted butter

2 large eggs

2 tbsp all-purpose
white flour

¼ tsp sea salt

½ cup walnuts or pecans

Tart shells
(recipe below)

Soak the raisins in the maple syrup for at least 1 hour, preferably overnight, in the refrigerator.

Preheat oven to 350°F.

Cream the butter and brown sugar. Lightly beat the eggs, then add them to the butter–brown-sugar mixture. Fold in the maple syrup and raisins. Stir in the flour and sea salt.

Scoop the mixture to fill tart shells ¾ full; top each with a walnut or pecan.

Bake for 20 minutes or until golden brown.

TART SHELLS

Makes 12 to 16 tart shells

½ cup cold butter

2 cups all-purpose white
or whole wheat flour

½ tsp sea salt

½ cup cold water

Preheat oven to 350°F.

Cut the butter into small cubes. Mix the flour, butter, and sea salt in a bowl with your hand or in a food processor. Add the water and continue to mix just until the dough shapes into a ball.

Place parchment paper on the counter and sprinkle with additional flour. Cut the dough in half. Roll out on the parchment paper. Cut circles to fit your muffin or tart pans. Place in the pans. Bake 10 minutes, and allow to cool.

BONITA'S TIPS
Always make pastry with cold butter; place pastry in the refrigerator after forming a ball to cool before rolling out.

PUMPKIN SPICE CREAM CHEESE PIE

Makes one 9-inch pie

9-inch pie crust
(see recipe page 71)

Cream cheese filling
8 oz cream cheese

¼ cup icing sugar

1 tsp vanilla

1 tbsp evaporated milk

Pumpkin spice filling
1½ cups mashed
pumpkin (prepare the day
before; see method below)

2 large eggs

¼ cup evaporated milk

2 tbsp all-purpose
white flour

1 tsp cinnamon

⅛ tsp cloves

1 tsp ginger

⅛ tsp pepper

½ tsp nutmeg

½ tsp sea salt

1 cup white sugar

Preheat oven to 350°F.

Prepare pumpkin: Clean a small sugar pumpkin by cutting it in half and removing the seeds and stringy bits. Cover a cookie sheet with parchment paper. Place the pumpkin, cut side down, on the sheet. Bake at 350°F for 60 minutes.

Let the pumpkin cool, then scoop out the flesh into a strainer over a bowl. Put a plate on the pumpkin to help release all the liquid; let strain 6 to 8 hours or overnight. Reserve 1½ cups of the strained pumpkin for this recipe; scoop the rest into small bags and freeze.

BONITA'S TIPS

If you are using salted butter, do not add salt to the pie crust dough.

Bake the pumpkin the day before you make the pie.

To roast the pumpkin seeds, clean them, sprinkle with spices of choice, and roast at 350°F for 60 minutes.

Make pie crust: Roll out half of the pastry and pat into a greased pie pan. Do not bake.

Make cream cheese filling: Beat all ingredients and spread over the uncooked pie shell.

Make pumpkin spice filling: Use a hand or stand mixer at low speed to combine all the ingredients. Spread over the cream cheese filling.

Bake 30 minutes at 350°F, then at 375°F for another 30 minutes. Check for doneness by inserting a knife into the centre of the pie; if it comes out clean, remove the pie from the oven and cool.

**Easter Pudding with
White Cream Sauce**

OTHER DESSERTS

APPLE FLIPS

Makes 8 flips

Pastry
1 cup butter

½ cup white sugar

1 tsp vanilla

¼ cup evaporated milk
or heavy cream

2 large eggs

2½ cups all-purpose
white flour

2 tsp baking powder

Pinch sea salt

Apple filling
3 apples of choice

½ tsp cloves

½ tsp nutmeg

1 tsp cinnamon

1 tsp lemon juice

½ cup brown sugar

Preheat oven to 350°F.

In a medium bowl, cream the butter, sugar, vanilla, milk, and eggs. Sift in the flour, baking powder, and sea salt and mix thoroughly.

When the dough becomes too hard to move with the spoon, use your hand to continue to work the dough until it forms a ball. Cover the dough with plastic wrap, then place in the refrigerator for about 15 minutes while you prepare the apples.

Peel the apples and cut into small pieces. Place in a bowl and toss with the spices, lemon juice, and brown sugar.

Remove the dough from the refrigerator. Dust the counter with flour and roll the dough to about ⅛ inch thick. Use a 6-inch diameter bowl or pastry cutter to cut 8 pastry rounds, re-rolling as necessary.

Place 3 teaspoons of the apple mixture on one half of each round. Fold the dough to cover the filling and pinch the sides with a fork to seal.

Line a cookie sheet with parchment paper. Place the apple flips on the cookie sheet at least 1 inch apart. Use a fork to poke holes in the top of each apple flip. Brush with melted butter.

Bake 20 to 25 minutes or until golden brown.

Serve hot or cold alone or with whipped cream or ice cream.

BAKED PARTRIDGEBERRY PUDDING

Makes 1 pudding

1 cup liquid from canned chickpeas

2 tbsp sugar

½ cup butter

¼ cup white sugar

2 large eggs

½ tsp vanilla

2 cups all-purpose white flour

1 tsp baking powder

Pinch sea salt

½ cup partridgeberries, fresh or frozen

Preheat oven to 350°F.

In a small bowl, beat the chickpea liquid at high speed until it forms peaks. Add 2 tablespoons sugar and continue beating until soft peaks form.

In a second bowl, cream the butter and ¼ cup sugar. Mix continuously while adding one egg at a time, then the vanilla.

Sift 1¾ cups of the flour, baking powder, and salt into the butter mixture. Fold in the beaten chickpea liquid.

Toss the partridgeberries with the remaining ¼ cup flour. Add to the batter and stir until the berries are well incorporated. Grease an 8 x 4½-inch pudding bowl (or a round deep pan, ideally with a lid).

Pour the batter into the bowl and cover with a lid or foil. Bake for 30 minutes covered and 30 minutes uncovered, until golden brown.

BONITA'S TIPS
This partridgeberry pudding is high in fibre due to the chickpea liquid. You can substitute 1 cup evaporated or fresh milk.

You can also steam this pudding in a pot of hot water. For details, follow the recipe at bonitaskitchen.com for boiled steamed puddings.

BLUEBERRY BREAD PUDDING WITH **CARAMEL SAUCE**

Makes 8–10 servings

6 cups homemade bread, cubed

1¼ cups evaporated milk or cream

3 large eggs

¼ cup brown sugar or honey

2 tbsp vanilla

1 cup blueberries, fresh or frozen

2 tsp ground cinnamon

3 tbsp melted butter

Caramel sauce
(recipe below)

Preheat oven to 350°F.

Soak the bread cubes in the milk in a large mixing bowl, folding until the milk is absorbed.

In a separate bowl, beat the eggs, sugar, vanilla, and cinnamon. Gently stir into the bread mixture. Fold in the blueberries.

Pour the butter into a 9 x 13-inch baking pan. Ensure that the bottom and the sides of the pan are well coated with butter.

Pour the bread mixture into the pan and bake 35 minutes. When the pudding starts to brown and pull away from the edge of the pan, remove it from the oven.

Serve with caramel sauce.

CARAMEL SAUCE

2 tbsp butter

1 cup dark brown sugar

1 tbsp vanilla

¼ cup evaporated milk

Melt the butter in a saucepan. Add the sugar and vanilla and whisk to blend. Cook over low heat, stirring constantly just until the mixture thickens. **Do not allow it to simmer; it may curdle.** Remove from the heat and whisk in the milk. Whisk the caramel sauce before serving—the sauce should be soft, creamy, and smooth.

BONITA'S TIPS
This is best eaten the day it is made. Warm leftovers in the microwave.

BLUEBERRY COBBLER

Makes 1 cobbler

Filling

3 cups blueberries, fresh or frozen

1 cup white sugar

1 tsp lemon juice

Pinch lemon zest

1 tbsp all-purpose white flour

Batter

1 cup butter

½ cup white sugar

1 tsp vanilla

2 large eggs, beaten

½ cup evaporated milk or heavy cream

2 cups all-purpose white flour

2 tsp baking powder

Pinch sea salt

Preheat oven to 350°F.

In small bowl, toss the blueberries, sugar, lemon juice, zest, and flour. Spread the mixture in a greased 8-inch square pan or 9-inch round pie pan.

In a medium bowl, use a wooden spoon or hand mixer to combine the butter, sugar, vanilla, eggs, and cream. Sift in the flour, baking powder, and salt and continue mixing the batter until thoroughly combined.

Spread the batter over the blueberries by dolloping or smoothing the top using a wooden spoon.

Bake for 40 to 45 minutes or until golden brown. Remove from the oven and cover with foil. Let set 15 to 20 minutes.

Serve with whipped cream or ice cream.

BONITA'S TIPS

If you are using frozen blueberries, there is no need to thaw them.

For easy mixing, use room temperature or partly melted butter when making the batter.

BLUEBERRY SHORTCAKE

Makes one 9-inch round cake

Batter

1 cup salted butter

½ cup white sugar

2 large eggs

1½ tsp vanilla

2 cups all-purpose white flour

1½ tsp baking powder

1 cup evaporated milk, room temperature

Blueberry sauce

2 cups fresh or frozen blueberries

2 tbsp cornstarch

3 tbsp white sugar

1 tbsp lemon juice

Whipped cream

1 cup whipping cream

2 tbsp icing sugar

½ cup blueberries for garnish

Preheat oven to 350°F.

Make batter: In a large bowl, cream the butter and sugar. Add the eggs, one at a time, stirring continuously. Add the vanilla. Mix until light and fluffy.

Sift the flour and baking powder into the butter mixture and stir to combine. Slowly mix in the evaporated milk. Fold in the blueberries.

Pour the batter into a greased, 9-inch springform pan or a pie dish. Bake for 45 to 60 minutes or until a toothpick or knife inserted in the middle of the cake comes out dry.

Remove the cake from the oven and let it sit in the pan for 5 to 10 minutes. Remove and set on a cooling rack.

Make blueberry sauce: Combine the blueberries, cornstarch, sugar, and lemon juice in a small saucepan. Cook on medium heat for 5 to 7 minutes, remove from the heat, and cool to room temperature on the counter or over a bowl of ice.

Whip cream: Whip the cold whipping cream until light and fluffy. Mix in the icing sugar.

Layer blueberry shortcake: Place the cake on a platter. Top with the blueberry sauce. Spread the whipped cream over the blueberries.

Garnish with fresh blueberries. Refrigerate for at least 1 hour before serving.

EASTER PUDDING WITH WHITE CREAM SAUCE

Makes 1 pudding

½ cup butter

⅓ cup white sugar

2 cups all-purpose white flour

2 tsp baking powder

Pinch sea salt

¼ tsp nutmeg

2 large eggs

1 cup evaporated milk

½ tsp vanilla

½ tsp almond extract

½ tsp orange zest

½ cup dried mixed fruit

⅓ cup raisins

1 tbsp lemon zest

Preheat oven to 350°F.

In a medium bowl, cream the butter and sugar. Sift 1¾ cups of the flour, baking powder, and sea salt into the butter mixture; reserve ¼ cup of the flour to toss with the mixed fruit.

Combine the eggs, milk, vanilla, and almond extract. Add to the butter-flour mixture and mix thoroughly. Fold the orange zest and mixed fruit into the batter.

Grease a pudding bowl or a round, deep pan. Pour the batter into the bowl or pan and bake uncovered for 1 hour or until golden brown.

You can also steam this pudding. Cover the pudding bowl and place in a boiler filled about one-quarter full with boiling water. Let steam for 90 minutes.

2 tbsp butter

½ cup milk

½ cup warm water

⅓ cup white sugar

2 tbsp all-purpose
white flour or cornstarch

⅛ tsp nutmeg

½ tsp almond extract

½ tsp orange zest

½ tsp lemon zest

WHITE CREAM SAUCE

In a small saucepan, warm the butter, milk, water, and sugar while stirring.

Combine the flour with ¼ cup cold water in a Mason jar. Shake until the lumps are gone. Pour the liquid from the jar into the saucepan slowly, stirring until the mixture thickens. Remove from the heat. Stir continuously while adding the nutmeg, almond extract, and zest.

Pour sauce over the hot pudding.

LEMON PUDDING

Makes one 9-inch square pudding

Filling

3 tbsp cornstarch

3 tbsp all-purpose white flour

½ cup white sugar

1½ cups boiling water

4 tbsp lemon juice

Zest of 1 or 2 lemons

2 tsp butter

3 egg yolks

Preheat oven to 350°F.

Make filling: In a large saucepan, combine the cornstarch, flour, and sugar. Place over medium heat and slowly add 1 cup boiling water while stirring. Cook for 2 minutes. Add the lemon juice, lemon zest, and butter, stirring continuously.

In a small bowl, lightly whisk the egg yolks. Slowly add ⅓ cup of the hot lemon liquid to them while whisking. Pour the yolk mixture into the saucepan and continue whisking. When thoroughly combined, remove the saucepan from the heat, add ½ cup boiling water, and stir. Set aside to cool to room temperature.

Batter

½ cup butter

½ cup white sugar

2 cups sifted all-purpose white flour

1 tsp vanilla

2 large eggs

2 tsp baking powder

Pinch sea salt

¾ cup evaporated milk

Make batter: In a medium bowl, cream the butter and sugar. Add the vanilla, eggs, and milk and mix thoroughly. Sift the flour, baking powder, and sea salt into the mixture; combine.

Grease a 9 x 9-inch pan. Smooth the batter in the bottom of the pan; pour the lemon filling over the top. Bake 40 to 45 minutes or until golden brown.

Serve with whipped cream or thick cream.

BONITA'S TIPS

Use fresh lemons for best flavour.

Add more boiling water if the lemon filling is too thick before spreading over the cake batter.

You may substitute the 2 eggs in the batter with 3 egg whites.

MERINGUE BOWLS WITH RHUBARB-BERRY FILLING

Makes 6 bowls

Meringue
3 egg whites
¾ cup icing sugar
1 tbsp cornstarch
1 tsp white vinegar
1 tsp vanilla

Rhubarb-berry filling
5 sticks rhubarb, chopped
1 cup mixed berries
¼ cup brown sugar
1 tsp orange zest
1 tsp cornstarch
¼ cup water

Topping
1 cup whipping cream
1 tbsp icing sugar
Fresh berries

BONITA'S TIPS
For best results, at 30 minutes, turn oven off—**do not open the oven door**—and let the meringue bowls cool completely in the oven for 90 minutes.

Make meringue bowls: Preheat oven to 250°F. Line a cookie sheet with parchment paper.

In a medium bowl, beat the egg whites with a hand mixer until soft peaks form.

Combine the icing sugar and cornstarch and add to the egg whites, 1 tablespoon at a time, while beating. Add the vanilla and vinegar, and beat to combine.

Use a small drop of egg white mixture at each corner of the parchment paper to stick it to the cookie sheet.

Scoop 6 equal mounds of meringue onto the parchment paper, spreading each first into a disk and then forming into a bowl. Bake 30 minutes.

Make rhubarb-berry filling: Combine all ingredients in a medium saucepan and bring to a boil over medium heat. Cook until the mixture starts to condense and thicken. Remove from the heat and let cool.

Make topping: Whip the cream. Add the icing sugar and whip to combine.

To serve, place each meringue bowl on a plate. Fill with the rhubarb-berry filling and top with the whipped cream and additional berries.

PEACH COBBLER

Makes 1 cobbler

Filling
6 to 8 fresh peaches

1 to 2 tbsp butter

1 cup brown sugar

1 tsp lemon zest

1 tsp cinnamon

Batter
½ cup butter,
room temperature

½ cup white sugar

1 tsp vanilla

½ cup evaporated milk
or heavy cream

2 large eggs

2 cups all-purpose
white flour

2 tsp baking powder

Pinch sea salt

Preheat oven to 350°F.

Peel peaches by placing them, two at a time, into a hot water bath for 1 minute, then immediately into an ice bath. Peel with a paring knife and cut into wedges, removing the stones.

Melt the better in a deep, oven-safe frying pan, ideally cast iron. Add the peach wedges. Fry for a few minutes, flipping partway through. Add the brown sugar, lemon zest, and cinnamon. Stir gently to combine and remove from the heat.

In a medium bowl, cream the butter, sugar, vanilla, eggs, and milk. Sift in the flour, baking powder, and salt. Mix thoroughly.

Scoop the batter on top of the peaches and spread evenly.

Bake for 40 to 45 minutes or until golden brown.

Serve with thick cream, whipped cream, or ice cream.

BONITA'S TIPS
Crack the eggs in a separate bowl to check for shells.

Frozen peaches can be used for this recipe; thaw first and follow the method above.